PANDAS

WILLOW CLARK

PowerKiDS
press™

New York

Published in 2013 by The Rosen Publishing Group, Inc.
29 East 21st Street, New York, NY 10010

First Edition

Editor: Joanne Randolph
Book Design: Ashley Drago

Photo Credits: Cover Frank Lukasseck/Photographer's Choice/Getty Images; pp. 4, 5, 8, 14, 15, 18 Shutterstock.com; pp. 7, 12 Fuse/Getty Images; p. 9 Stan Osolinski/Taxi/Getty Images; p. 10 © www.iStockphoto.com/Norman Chan; p. 11 PhotoTalk/Vetta/Getty Images; pp. 13, 19 (right) iStockphoto/Thinkstock; p. 13 (right) Keren Su/Stone/Getty Images; p. 16 John Giustina/Taxi/Getty Images; p. 17 Danita Delimont/Gallo Images/Getty Images; pp. 20, 22 Keren Su/China Span/Getty Images; p. 21 (right) Gary Vestal/Photographer's Choice/Getty Images; p. 21 (left) AFP/Getty Images.

Library of Congress Cataloging-in-Publication Data

Clark, Willow.
 Pandas / by Willow Clark. — 1st ed.
   p. cm. — (The animals of Asia)
 Includes index.
 ISBN 978-1-4488-7414-9 (library binding) — ISBN 978-1-4488-7487-3 (pbk.) —
ISBN 978-1-4488-7561-0 (6-pack)
 1. Pandas—Juvenile literature. I. Title.
 QL737.C27C585 2013
 599.789—dc23
                              2011049391

Manufactured in China

CPSIA Compliance Information: Batch #WKTS12PK: For Further Information contact Rosen Publishing, New York, New York at 1-800-237-9932

CONTENTS

HELLO, PANDA!

When you hear the word "panda," you might think first of the black-and-white giant panda. This member of the bear family has come to stand for the movement to help **endangered** animals.

Giant pandas spend much of their days eating bamboo.

Red pandas are much smaller than giant pandas. They are most active in the late afternoon, night, and early morning hours.

You may also have heard of the red panda. Although it has a similar name to the giant panda, the red panda is more closely related to raccoons than it is to bears. Both the giant panda and the red panda live in bamboo forests in the mountains of Asia. This book will tell you more about these Asian animals.

IN THE MOUNTAINS OF ASIA

Giant pandas live in mountainous areas in central China in the Sichuan, Gansu, and Shanxi Provinces. This **habitat** is cool and wet and has forests where lots of bamboo grows. Giant pandas once lived in the lowlands of these areas.

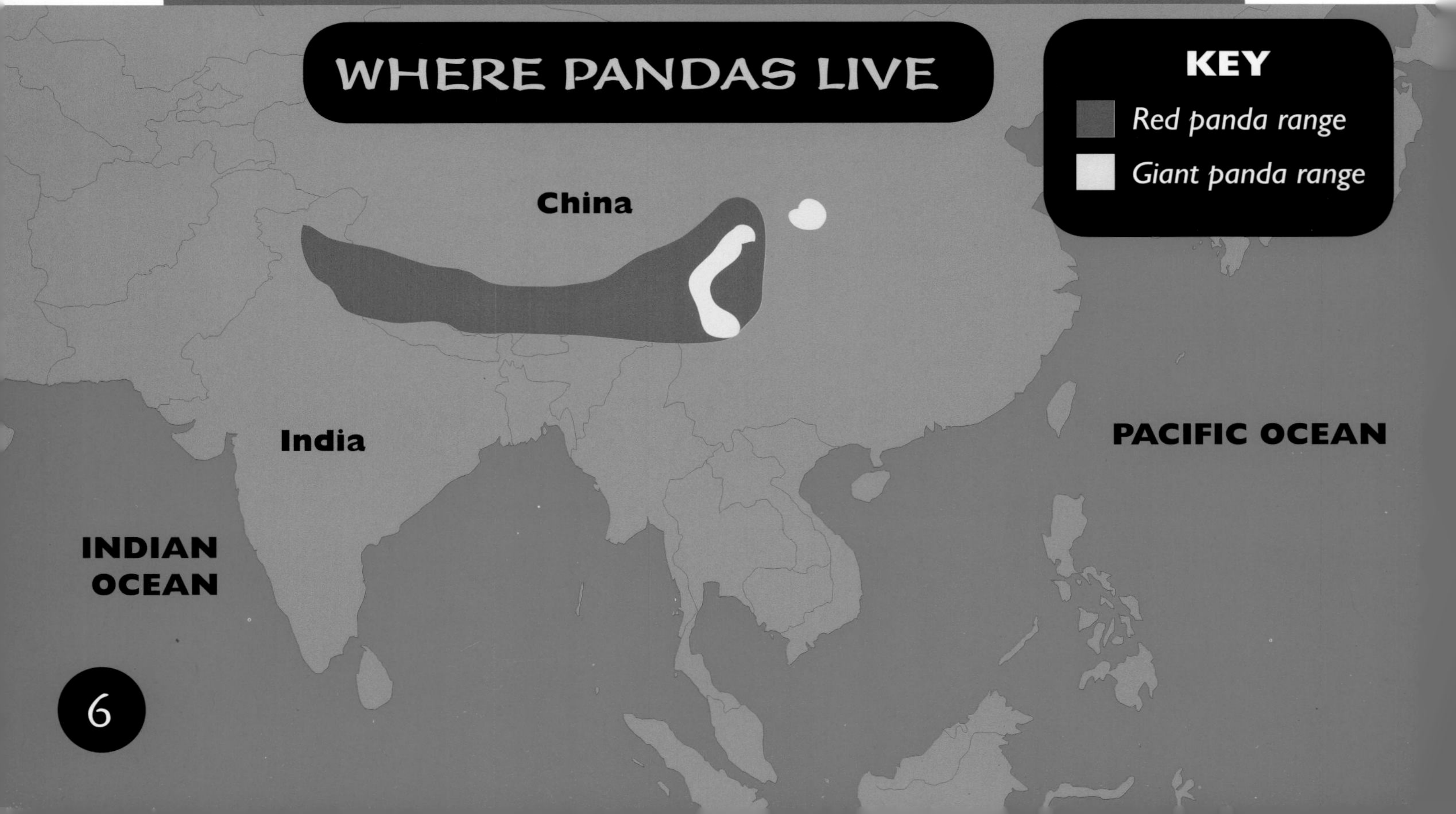

WHERE PANDAS LIVE

KEY

Red panda range

Giant panda range

China

India

PACIFIC OCEAN

INDIAN OCEAN

Farming and forest clearing have pushed the giant panda farther up into the mountains, though.

Red pandas are found throughout the cool, mountainous forests in the countries of Nepal, India, Bhutan, and Myanmar. They also live in the mountainous forests of China's Sichuan and Yunnan Provinces, where their range overlaps with that of the giant panda.

◀ *Giant pandas eat shade-loving or forest bamboo species that grow best on wet, cool mountainsides. People plant sun-loving bamboo that grows in clumps in open places.*

THE TWO PANDAS

Scientists have studied the giant panda and the red panda to figure out if the two **species** are related. They also want to know to which other animals they are related. Sorting animals in this way is called classification. Studies of the giant

Giant pandas look a lot like other bears. This gave scientists a clue as to where to start when classifying this panda.

▲ People thought red pandas were related to raccoons because of the white masks on their faces and the rings on their tails.

panda's genetic code have led scientists to group this animal with the bear family.

Red pandas were once thought to be part of the raccoon family because their bodies looked similar to raccoons'. They were also once classified with the bear family. Scientists have since decided that red pandas do not have any close living relatives. Today they are in a family all by themselves!

YUMMY BAMBOO

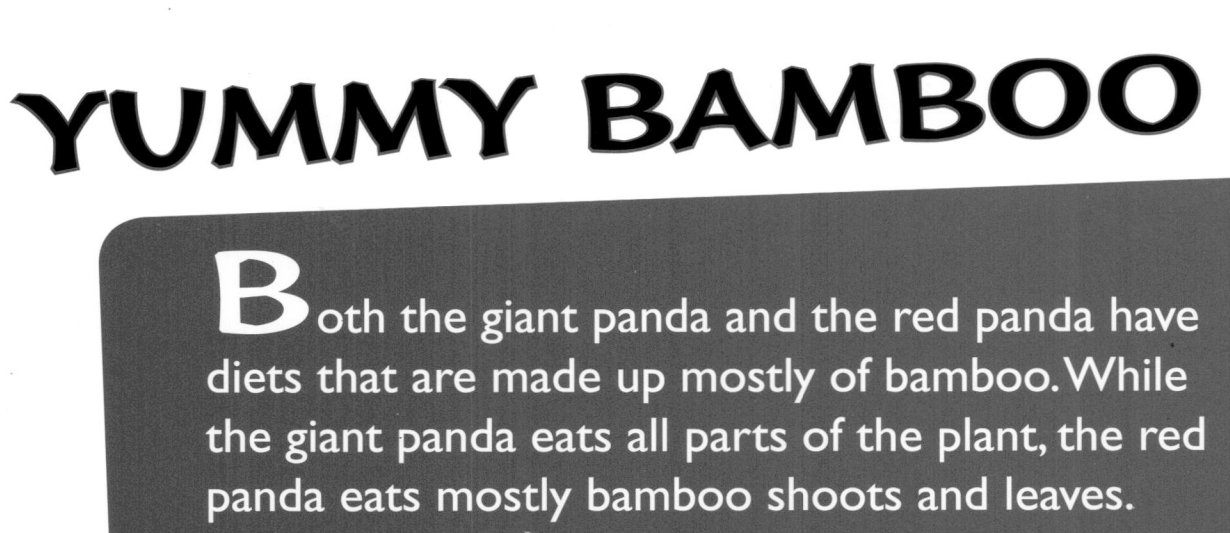

Both the giant panda and the red panda have diets that are made up mostly of bamboo. While the giant panda eats all parts of the plant, the red panda eats mostly bamboo shoots and leaves.

Red pandas eat a lot of bamboo, but they also eat other things. The red pandas' diet includes fruit, flowers, acorns, eggs, and small animals. ▼

▲ *Most of what is in the bamboo is passed in the giant panda's waste. The giant panda goes to the bathroom dozens of times each day!*

Bamboo is plentiful and grows year-round, but it does not have many **nutrients**. Pandas must eat lots of bamboo. In fact, giant pandas eat about 28 pounds (13 kg) of bamboo every day! Finding and eating bamboo takes up 10 to 16 hours of the red panda's and the giant panda's day. They spend the rest of their time resting or sleeping.

AT HOME IN THE FOREST

Red pandas and giant pandas have **adaptations** that help them live in a forest habitat. Both pandas have "false thumbs." These are large wrist bones that are covered by pads of skin. They use these bones to hold on to bamboo. Both kinds of pandas

Red pandas use their false thumbs to help them climb and to grip bamboo. ▼

are skillful tree climbers with sharp claws to grip tree branches.

Giant pandas have thick, woolly fur that keeps them warm in wet, chilly weather. Red pandas have long tails. Their long tails help them balance as they move along branches. They also use these bushy tails like blankets when the weather is cold.

Giant pandas do not have long bushy tails, but they do have thick fur that keeps them warm. ▼

Red pandas have tails that are about as long as the rest of their bodies. They can cover themselves with them while they sleep in their cool habitat. ▲

THE RED PANDA

The red panda's body is about the size of a cat's, with a tail that is about the same length as its body. Its fur blends in with the colors of its forest surroundings. Coloring that helps an animal blend with its surroundings is called **camouflage**.

Red pandas are around 25 inches (63.5 cm) long and their tails are around 19 inches (48 cm) long.

Red pandas have reddish fur on their backs and black fur on their legs. Their faces can have white, brown, black, or red fur and markings.

Red pandas are most active between dusk and dawn. During the night, they look for food throughout their territories. The territories of individual red pandas often overlap, but they are **solitary** animals. This means that they live alone unless they are **mating** or raising babies. Red pandas communicate by marking territory, through body language, and by making sounds.

15

THE GIANT PANDA

The giant panda is between 4 and 6 feet (1–2 m) long, which is about the size of an American black bear. Scientists are not sure why the giant panda has its black-and-white coloring. They think that it may help camouflage giant pandas or help them attract mates.

One way giant pandas tell other animals that they should go away is by staring at them. Some scientists think the black spots around giant pandas' eyes help with this defense.

Like red pandas, giant pandas are solitary animals. They tend to stay away from one another unless it is mating season. They communicate mostly through marking territory and by making sounds. Unlike other bears, giant pandas do not make loud, growling noises. Instead they make noises like barks, huffs, and bleats.

Unlike many other bear species, the giant panda does not hibernate. Giant pandas are active even in snowy, cold weather. ▶

PANDA PREDATORS

Adult giant pandas have few **predators**. They are sometimes hunted by snow leopards, though. Yellow-throated martens sometimes eat giant panda cubs. Giant pandas do their best to try to stay away from predators. If they cannot escape, then they will fight back.

Snow leopards eat mainly sheep and goats but have been known to eat red pandas and giant panda cubs as well. ▼

Snow leopards and martens also hunt red pandas. When red pandas feel threatened, they try to escape by climbing into the trees. They may also release strong scents from glands near their tails. If getting away is not possible, they will stand on their back legs and use their sharp front claws to strike out at predators.

A marten is part of the weasel family. Yellow-necked martens sometimes eat panda cubs, in addition to birds, small animals, deer, and fruits.

BABY PANDAS

Both giant pandas and red pandas mate only once every couple of years. Red pandas mate in the winter and have litters of one to four cubs in the late spring. Giant pandas mate in the spring and have one or two cubs in the summer.

Baby giant panda

The red panda's life span is between 8 and 10 years, while the giant panda's is between 14 and 20 years.

Giant panda mothers play with their cubs. Sometimes a mother even wakes up her cub to get it to play!

Giant panda and red panda cubs are blind and helpless when they are born. Their mothers **nurse** them until they can start eating bamboo. At about 18 months, both giant panda and red panda mothers force their young to leave. While red pandas are adults at this age, giant pandas are not full-grown adults until between the ages of four and eight.

PANDAS IN TROUBLE

Both giant pandas and red pandas are in trouble. Giant pandas are endangered. There are only about 1,000 to 1,600 living in the wild, and about 100 more live in zoos. Red pandas are **vulnerable**, meaning they are at risk for becoming endangered.

The biggest threat to pandas is habitat loss. **Poachers** are another threat pandas face. **Conservation** groups are encouraging countries where pandas live to make and enforce laws that protect the animals and their habitats. Such protections will help these Asian animals continue to survive in the wild.

▲ To help save the endangered giant panda, China set aside 494,211 acres (200,000 ha) of land as a nature reserve. This mother and her cub make their home in this protected area.

GLOSSARY

ADAPTATIONS (a-dap-TAY-shunz) Changes in an animal that help it stay alive.

CAMOUFLAGE (KA-muh-flahj) A color or shape that matches what is around something and helps hide it.

CONSERVATION (kon-sur-VAY-shun) Protecting something from harm.

ENDANGERED (in-DAYN-jerd) In danger of no longer existing.

HABITAT (HA-buh-tat) The surroundings where an animal or a plant naturally lives.

MATING (MAYT-ing) Coming together to make babies.

NURSE (NURS) When a female feeds her baby milk from her body.

NUTRIENTS (NOO-tree-ents) Food that a living thing needs to live and grow.

POACHERS (POH-cherz) People who illegally kill animals that are protected by the law.

PREDATORS (PREH-duh-terz) Animals that kill other animals for food.

SOLITARY (SAH-leh-ter-ee) Spending most time alone.

SPECIES (SPEE-sheez) One kind of living thing. All people are one species.

VULNERABLE (VUL-neh-ruh-bel) Could be easily hurt.

INDEX

WEBSITES

Due to the changing nature of Internet links, PowerKids Press has developed an online list of websites related to the subject of this book. This site is updated regularly. Please use this link to access the list:
www.powerkidslinks.com/aoa/pand/